MW00961790

1

First published in the United States in 2020 by
MAGIC PARENTING MEDIA
MagicParenting.com

Copyright © 2020 by Alexandra Clark and Nicolas Mottet
ISBN: 9781710017250

All rights reserved. No part of this publication may be repro-
duced, stored or transmitted in any form or by any means elec-
tronic, mechanical, photocopying, or otherwise, without the prior
permission of the copyright owner.

The right of Alexandra Clark and Nicolas Mottet to be identified
as authors of this work has been asserted by them in accordance
with the Copyright, Designs and Patents Act, 1988.

Magic Mom,
Magic Dad

Thirty years of research turned into simple cartoons to help parents with young children (ages 2-5) avoid temper tantrums.

Follow us on instagram:
instagram.com/magic_mom_magic_dad

Follow us on Facebook:
facebook.com/MagicMomMagicDad

About the authors

Alexandra Clark, Ph.D., is a neuroscience researcher and former director of a music school for young children. She has published a number of scholarly articles on music, memory and psychology. She lives in Seattle with her husband and three children. She holds a Ph.D. from Northwestern University.

Nicolas Mottet, MBA, has worked for the past ten years for Amazon, most recently as a Principal Product Manager. He lives in Seattle with his wife and three children. He holds an MBA from the Kellogg School of Management at Northwestern University.

With special thanks to:

Nancy Malsawmthar, a cartoonist who has published several books and cartoons for children.

Hélène Martins, a project manager who has also worked as a nanny, caring for three young children.

To Chloé, Sophie and Sébastien
who inspired many of the stories in this book.

CONTENTS

Thirty years of research turned into simple cartoons to help parents with young children (ages 2-5) avoid temper tantrums.

MAGIC WAY 6: How to use time-outs and discipline

INTRODUCTION

Why Magic Mom, Magic Dad?

Magic Mom, Magic Dad presents findings from scientific research in a simple cartoon format to help parents better communicate with young children (ages 2 to 5) to avoid temper tantrums. Most parents don't have time to read through hundreds of pages of text from a book. The few who do will find it hard to remember anything from the information overload.

Magic Mom, Magic Dad distills the most important learnings into cartoons that can be read in less than 60 minutes. We published this book because we believe that there is a wealth of information and research that can benefit parents but it was not available in an easily consumable format, until now. We believe that simple cartoons, known for their entertainment value, are easier to read and provide practical information that parents can use right away to avoid tantrums, re-gain sanity, and develop a positive and fulfilling bond with their children.

MAGIC WAY 1

First, connect with your child

The first step to successfully manage tantrums with young children is to connect with them emotionally and help them realize that you understand how they feel. Children having tantrums might appear unreasonable and stubborn, but that is precisely when they need you the most. Once children feel that their parents are on their side and understand them, they are able to become calmer and are more open to finding solutions to their problems.

For this Magic Way, you will find 4 cartoons describing how to best connect with your child in a challenging situation. Connecting with children means that we understand their feelings (cartoon 1), give them our full attention and love (cartoons 2 & 3), and empathize with them to show that we are on their side (cartoon 4).

Cartoons for this Magic Way:

Cartoon 1: Understand your child's feelings.

Cartoons 2 & 3: Give your child full attention (two examples: at home and at the park).

Cartoon 4: Empathize with your child's feelings.

Cartoon 1

Understand your child's feelings

"Peaceful parenting is simply treating our tiny humans with the same humanity that we like to be treated with ourselves."
LR Knost

Research behind the cartoon:

Effective communication between parents and children is the cornerstone of a healthy relationship. Such communication requires that parents become aware of and understand their children's feelings and emotions. Parents who empathize and connect emotionally with their children are more likely to enjoy deep and meaningful relationships. According to research by the Gottman Research Institute[1] (2019), this parenting approach involves five essential ingredients:

1) awareness of emotions,
2) connecting,
3) listening,
4) naming emotions, and
5) finding solutions.

Parents who connect with children in this way build emotional intelligence in their children. Of course, connecting and having meaningful communication with children, in addition to understanding their feelings and emotions, is not always as easy as it sounds. In some cases, parents will have to navigate working through a child's reluctance to talk about their feelings without pushing too hard, which can result in the child shutting down. Non-communicative children often want the help and support of their parents, but sometimes have trouble verbalizing their feelings. Working with children so they can recognize the vast array of emotions they may experience (e.g., happiness, sadness, anger, frustration, etc) is important to this method's success.

Parents should 1) detect when a child gets frustrated ("awareness of emotions"), and 2) understand how to gently nudge for more information to better understand the situation and connect with the child (in cartoon: "You seem very upset. Did something bad happen at school?"). This helps parents understand their child's emotions and feelings so that they can respond accordingly.

When parents approach such situations with warmth and empathy, children learn that their parents are always there for them. This positive parenting style is not always easy, especially when frustrated kids express feelings in an indirect way, for example with urgent wants and needs that may be out of the question (in cartoon: "I want to go to the park now!!"). In the heat of the moment, a parent's first impulse might be to deny the child's requests without realizing the underlying reasons for the behavior. This is a surefire way to build your child's resentment and (unknowingly) initiate a tantrum.

Instead, by being aware of children's emotions and using a supportive parenting style, parents acknowledge their children's needs and feelings (e.g., "Yes, that sounds fun, I understand why you are so interested in it"). When speaking to children with love and understanding, parents model a calm demeanor that teaches children emotion regulation. Ultimately, when children do open-up to parents by verbalizing their feelings, parents should recognize and encourage this behavior (in cartoon: "It's good that you are letting me know"), so that it is repeated many times in the future.

Key take-aways to understand your child's feelings:

1) Being aware of feelings: the sooner you understand something is wrong, the easier it will be for you to help.

2) Connecting & listening: gently nudge for more information (in cartoon: "Why don't you like school? Tell me how you feel").

3) Naming feelings: naming feelings and emotions in a sincere and caring way will show your child that you understand them and are on their side.

4) Encouraging sharing feelings: sharing current feelings will encourage proactive sharing in the future and helps build emotional intelligence and social skills (in cartoon: "It's good that you are letting me know").

Cartoon 1:
Understand your child's feelings
to avoid an argument

What to avoid

✱ The mom does not realize that her child is reacting
negatively because she is upset about school.
✱ The mom uses logical arguments that will not work well ("We just can't go now").
✱ She is quick to use commands ("Stop yelling"). This only
makes the situation worse.

What Magic Mom would do

✔ The mom recognizes that her child is upset.
✔ She connects and listens, by gently probing for more information.
✔ She names the feeling ("I see that you are sad") and
encourages sharing feelings.

Give your child full attention

"Your children need your presence more than your presents."
Jesse Jackson

Research behind the cartoon:

Giving children full attention with active listening is a very effective way to help children become calmer and re-gain their composure. Simple cues, both verbal and physical, can show children that they are truly being listened to and can help avoid tantrums. Once children feel that their parents are on their side, they are able to become calmer and are more open to finding and accepting new solutions.

When it comes to good parenting, actions often speak louder than words. It is simply not possible to provide children with the attention they need while multitasking. Children are keenly aware of whether they are truly being heard. Active listening means that parents are completely tuned-in to their children; it is reflected in both words and body language (in cartoon 2: "Here, sit down so you can tell me"). Listening with care and sensitivity shows kids that they are really being heard, and helps them calm down and focus on finding constructive solutions to their problems. Active listening by parents also promotes children's emotional resilience (Wolin et al., 2000[2]) and is a key aspect of developmental parenting, which is believed to support many positive child outcomes (Roggman et al., 2008[3]). Developmental parenting involves:

1) Affection, through positive expressions of warmth toward the children (sitting next to them, directly facing them, etc)

2) Responsiveness, by attending to children's cues, and

3) Encouragement, by supporting children's activities and interests.

The manner in which parents demonstrate affection, responsiveness and encouragement matters a lot. For example, by putting aside computers and other distractors (in cartoon 2), kneeling down to the children's heights (in cartoon 3) or simply positioning their body to face the children, parents show children that they are their first priority. Not only does this enhance a child's self-esteem and sense of worth, but it also models the behavior we want from our children. By tuning-in to children, parents help children develop healthy social habits and listening skills that facilitate positive relationships with both parents and peers alike.

This does not mean that children should always be allowed to interrupt their parents. For example, when parents need quiet time to work, they should first communicate and set expectations with their children to avoid interruptions. Children should be made aware that there are boundaries to respect and rules to follow (also see Magic Way 3: set rules and expectations ahead of time). However, in situations where a child needs help from parents, giving your child full attention, using both verbal and physical cues, can be very effective to avoid temper tantrums.

Key take-aways to give your child full attention:

1) Affection: demonstrate signs of affection through positive expressions of warmth, for example by inviting your child to sit next to you (in cartoon 2: "Here, sit down so you can tell me").

2) Responsiveness: give physical or verbal cues that you are giving your full attention, for example by putting your computer aside for a minute, or kneeling down to speak to your child.

3) Setting boundaries: giving your child your full attention does not mean that your child should always come first. Parents who need quiet time to get work done should firmly set expectations early with their children. Children need to be made aware that there are important boundaries to respect and rules to follow (also see Magic Way 3 for further recommendations on setting rules and expectations).

Cartoon 2
Give your child full attention (at home)

A girl wants to tell her dad about a problem at school. Her dad is busy working on his computer. How can the dad best respond?

What to avoid

✖ The dad's body language signals that he is not really listening (he looks at his computer and doesn't turn around to face her).
✖ The child feels like she is not getting attention and reacts negatively.

What Magic Dad would do

✔ The dad shows signs of affection such as inviting
his child to sit next to him.
✔ He gives visual cues that he is giving full attention, by putting his computer
to sleep. As a result, his daughter responds positively and feels supported.

Cartoon 3
Give your child full attention (at the park)

A mom is chatting with a friend at the park, but her daughter comes to her to get her attention. How should the mom best respond?

What to avoid

✖ The mom is chatting with her friend, and doesn't give physical
or verbal cues that she is truly listening.
✖ The mom doesn't detect that her child is getting upset.

What Magic Mom would do

✔ The mom gives physical cues that she is listening by kneeling down.
✔ She acknowledges the child's feelings ("I see, my love. I'm sorry").
Once the mom has helped her child, she will be able to talk
to her friend again.

Cartoon 4:

Empathize with your child's feelings

*"Affirming words from moms and dads are like light switches.
Speak a word of affirmation at the right moment in a child's
life and it's like lighting up a whole roomful of possibilities."*
Gary Smalley

Research behind the cartoon:

After giving your child full attention (see cartoons 2 and 3), empathizing with and affirming your child's feelings is another important step to solving conflicts or avoiding tantrums. When children know that their parents are not only truly listening but also empathizing and affirming their feelings, they are better able to calm down and regain composure. This often helps avoid full-blown temper tantrums.

When children become upset about something that may not seem significant to parents (e.g., the destruction of a flower or loss of a toy), parents need to respect children's fears and concerns and not belittle them. Talking to children about their worries shows empathy and helps children verbalize their feelings (Durrant, 2016[4]). This is a situation with no place for criticism or sarcasm, both of which are hurtful to children. Instead, parents should seek to understand their children's feelings and describe them back to show that they understand them (in cartoon: "Flowers dying can be upsetting. Is that why you are upset?").

It is also important to value and acknowledge when children discuss their feelings by rewarding the behavior to encourage information sharing in the future (in cartoon: "You are so caring about living things! That is really nice!"). Indeed, parents raising compassionate children should be proud of this accomplishment. By providing recognition for such behaviors, parents increase children's self-efficacy and improve their likelihood of engaging in more social and healthy behaviors. This sensitive and responsive parenting has many wonderful benefits, such as more secure parent-child attachments, increased self-esteem, self-efficacy, and social development among children (Juffer, Bakermans-Kranenburg & Van Ijzendoorn, 2008; Laible, Carlo & Roesch, 2004[5]). Difficult conversations are also an opportunity for parents to act as positive emotional coaches who talk through tough issues instead of dismissing them. This also has the benefit of encouraging children's emotional development in the process.

Key take-aways to empathize with your child's feelings:

1) Encourage children to talk about their feelings, by asking questions (in cartoon: "Flowers dying can be upsetting. Is that why you are upset?").

2) Acknowledge feelings. Describe the feelings to show that you understand how they feel and are here to help (in cartoon: "Sometimes, people don't realize they are hurting the flowers. This makes me sad too").

3) Provide positive reinforcement to encourage sharing feelings. By providing recognition and validation, parents encourage these behaviors, which will help promote social development.

Cartoon 4:
Empathize with your child's feelings to defuse a tantrum

A 5-year old girl is sad because her younger sister killed flowers, and continues to be upset despite her mom's reassurance. How can the mom help her feel better?

What to avoid

✖ The mom gets frustrated by the child's reaction.
✖ She negates the child's feelings ("They are only flowers") instead of acknowledging these feelings and helping her child process the emotions. As a result, both the mom and the child end up very upset.

What Magic Mom would do

✔ The mom encourages her child to talk about her feelings.
✔ She acknowledges the feelings ("Flowers dying can be upsetting").
✔ She provides positive reinforcement ("You are so caring about other living things"). As a result, the daughter feels listened to and is able to calm down.

MAGIC WAY 2

Suggest FUN alternatives

After you connect with your child in a moment of crisis to show that you understand their feelings and are on their side (see Magic Way 1), another simple and extremely effective step to defusing a challenging situation is to offer fun alternatives that give your child options to choose from. Is your child upset because it's time to leave the playground and go home? Suggest a fun alternative such as racing to the next lamp pole (which is of course conveniently positioned on the way back home) or start doing the frog or the crab walk (toward home).

If children are not able or allowed to perform a specific activity, providing a couple of new and fun options can help them feel a sense of control. It also redirects their energy toward positive behaviors. Doing this allows children to see a positive path forward: it is time for fun again! It is a win-win situation for both parents and children. This is a very effective and essential tactic in a parenting toolkit. Instead of denying a child's request, offer them fun alternatives and options.

For this Magic Way, we will review how to use fun alternatives to avoid a tantrum (cartoon 5) and more specifically how to avoid a tantrum with a child who is 2 or 3-year old (cartoon 6). Then we will review how to avoid fights between two children struggling to share toys (cartoon 7).

Cartoons for this Magic Way:

Cartoon 5: Fun alternatives to avoid a tantrum (the rain).

Cartoon 6: Fun alternatives to avoid a tantrum with a 2 or 3-year old (the knife).

Cartoon 7: Fun alternatives to avoid fights.

Cartoons 5 & 6

Suggest fun alternatives to avoid tantrums

"If a child is to keep alive his inborn sense of wonder,
he needs the companionship of at least one adult who can
share it, rediscovering with him the joy, excitement,
and mystery of the world we live in."
Rachel Carson

Research behind the cartoon:

Sometimes kids have pretty strange ideas about fun activities, such as building a hut outside when it is pouring rain (see cartoon 5). When their requests are denied, they feel frustrated and angry that their wants and needs are - yet again - vetoed by unfair parents who keep telling them what to do. Rather than simply denying requests, parents need to direct children toward more appropriate interests and fun alternatives without breaking their spirits. In doing so, parents avoid the negative consequences of constantly denying requests (in cartoon 5: "I don't think you can. It is raining"), which may result in resentment toward parents, revenge to get back at parents, rebellion against parents, and retreat. Constant denying of requests can also have a negative impact on the child's self-esteem (Nelsen, 2006[6]).

Parents should show children that their ideas are valued (in cartoon 5: "It sounds like so much fun!") even when parents know that they will not be able to engage in their children's plans. Such situations are perfect examples of the 'incompatible alternative principle' (Kersey, 2006[7]) where parents provide children with a new behavior to substitute for the undesirable one. For example, parents could suggest building a hut inside, rather than outside in the rain. Parents skilled at finding fun alternatives are more likely to get the child's cooperation and, as a result, more likely to avoid tantrums.

Suggesting several fun alternatives or options (which are acceptable to the parent) is also effective because children feel a sense of empowerment and control when given choices. It is a win-win situation for both parents and children. Additionally, involving children in the decision-making process to find alternative options can teach them valuable problem-solving skills and increase their chances of accepting one of these new options. After all, since "children are born good, are altruistic and desire to do the right thing" (Godfrey, 2019[8]); respectfully guiding them in a win-win positive direction fosters cooperation.

It is even better if parents suggest activities that involve parental interaction (in cartoon 6: "Help me cut a piece of butter"). Positive involvement with parental participation builds lifelong memories and strong family connections. This supportive, involved parenting not only teaches social skills but it is also associated with positive school adjustment and reduced behavior issues[9] later in life. It is a creative and fun solution to short-term problems, that also has long-term benefits.

Key take-aways to suggest fun alternatives to avoid tantrums:

1) When a child makes an unreasonable request, your natural tendency might be to deny the request with a logical explanation (in cartoon 5: "I said no. If you get wet, you might get sick"). However, this approach will likely frustrate the child. Research also shows that it will build resentment toward the parent.

2) Instead, show true empathy. This shows the child how much you understand and relate to them (in cartoon 5: "I know how much you want to build a hut in the garden").

3) Show children that their ideas are valued (in cartoon 5: "That sounds like a lot of fun!"), even if what they are asking for might not be possible.

4) Provide children with new behaviors to substitute for the undesirable one. Children feel empowered when given choices. The key is to make it playful and fun (in cartoon 6: "You can use this knife and help me cut a piece of butter").

Cartoon 5:
Fun alternatives to avoid a tantrum (the rain)

A 4-year old boy really wants to build a hut outside but it's raining. The dad doesn't want him to go outside and get wet. How will the dad respond to help avoid a crisis?

What to avoid

✖ The dad denies the request with a logical explanation,
and doesn't show empathy.
✖ The dad suggests an alternative (the legos) but doesn't make it
fun and interesting enough.

What Magic Dad would do

✔ The dad shows true empathy. He first agrees with his child: in an imaginary world, it would be fantastic to build a hut outside in the rain!
✔ He values his child's idea ("It sounds like so much fun").
✔ He suggests an alternative AND makes it fun.

Daddy, I want to build a hut in the garden.

It's a cool idea. It's raining though.

Yeah but I want to go there now!

I know how much you want to build a hut in the garden. It sounds like so much fun.

I wish I had a magic wand to build a hut somewhere dry. Would you want a magic wand like that too?

Yes, I'd like a magic wand like that!

How about we build a hut right in your bedroom. You can even use your legos inside the hut!

Yes, let's go!

Cartoon 6:
Fun alternatives to avoid a tantrum
with a 2 or 3-year old (the knife)

A 3-year old girl is crying because she is not allowed to use a large knife that her father is using. How can the dad stop the tantrum with a fun alternative or distraction?

What Magic Dad would do

With younger children (2-3 years old), fun distractions can be
surprisingly effective and work a lot better than logical arguments.
These distractions work mostly for younger children, and
are less effective for older children (4-5 years old).

Fun alternative.
The dad focuses on what the child
"can" do instead of what she "can't" do.

You can use this knife and
help me cut a piece of butter.
Let's do it together!

Fun distraction.
The dad shows the young girl a
book or toy and makes it interesting.

Oh look at this book.
The elephant has
a big hat!

Fun toy.
The dad improvises and remembers
he found a doll under the couch earlier.

Do you know what I found this
morning? I found your doll!! Come
with me and I will show you.

Funny face.
The dad makes a funny face, before
finding a new activity for the child.

Look. Let me show you a funny face.

Suggest fun alternatives to avoid fights

"There is a little boy inside the man who is my brother...
Oh, how I hated that little boy. And how I love him too."
Rebecca Eanes

Research behind the cartoon:

Bickering children have been known to fray their parents' nerves. Oftentimes, parents are not sure how to deal with fights and, in an effort to simply make them stop, don't always make the most thoughtful decisions. For example, well-meaning parents may jump into their children's arguments as referees or judges, trying to determine "who started it" or "which toy belongs to whom." Excluding violent or dangerous conflicts, parenting experts suggest a different approach.

For example, the 'Love and Logic' method described by Cline and Faye[10] (2006) suggests that parents "just go brain dead" during conflicts. What they mean is that parents should not argue; but remain calm, show empathy, and express their love for their children. They suggest that parents might say: "I love you too much to argue." This does not mean giving-in; as 'Love and Logic' parenting is not permissive. Parent still need to make children accountable for behavior by understanding the consequences. But when these messages are communicated in a loving way, children are less likely to regard their parents as the enemy.

Similarly, noted positive parenting and sibling rivalry expert, Amy McCready[11] (2019), suggests that parents stay out of squabbles about who is right, unless absolutely necessary, and work with the children to find solutions. In doing so, parents are not reinforcing the disagreements, rather they are giving children the opportunity to work out solutions together (in cartoon: "Let's play with the yoga balls, and then find a solution together"). Parents are often surprised how well children can work out solutions without parents telling them what to do. McCready also suggests that parents put all children "in the same boat." In other words, rather than trying to negotiate "who did what," if all children involved in the conflict receive the same consequence, they learn that they each will benefit from getting along in the future (e.g., "If you both cannot play together with the toy, you will need to find something else to do"). When parental intervention is needed, it should be done calmly and without taking sides.

Distracting children with another fun activity or toy (in cartoon: the yoga balls or the volcano) is often helpful with younger children, as is modeling deep-breathing exercises that help calm the chaos. A cooling-off period is actually advantageous for both children and parents, who sometimes need to take a few breaths too! When both children and parents are more relaxed, they are better able to determine positive solutions and fun alternatives that will work for everyone.

Key take-aways to suggest fun alternatives to avoid fights:

1) Calmly interrupt the conflict to start addressing the problem. Engage the children with specific toys that are exclusively used to help reduce anger (in cartoon: "Max, Klara, let me show you something very cool"). Distracting children with another fun activity is often helpful, as is modeling deep-breathing exercises that help calm the chaos.

2) Do not take sides. If children cannot work out a solution, put all children "in the same boat": if all children involved in the conflict get the same consequence, they learn that they will benefit from getting along in the future.

3) Do not argue. Parents should remain calm and show empathy.

4) Encourage children to work out solutions together (in cartoon: "We're going to relax, and then find a solution"). If they are old enough, you can even ask them to come up with a solution. You might be surprised how often children are able to find a solution you had not considered.

5) Find fun alternatives to help children step away from the conflict to focus on a more positive activity.

Cartoon 7:
Fun alternatives to avoid fights

What Magic Mom would do (part 1/2)

✔ The mom calmly interrupts the conflict and calms children
with an interesting fun activity.
✔ She sets a path for the children to be able to work out a solution.

Part 1/2...

What Magic Mom would do (part 2/2)

✔ The mom continues to help the children calm
down with short breathing exercises.
✔ She comes up with a fun solution, the volcano, that sounds
even more fun than the original game. She could also
have asked the children to come up with a solution.

...part 2/2

Hold your ball, and inhale deeply.
Then exhale to release tension...

Yes, mommy.

Now that you are both feeling more calm,
let's find a solution for the puzzle.
Can we do that?

Yes, mom.

Can you play this puzzle together?

No, I started
it first.

No, I want to play
with it alone.

I have a solution. You can take turns. Max,
how about we play with this very cool
volcano together while Klara starts her
turn for 5 minutes with the puzzle?

Ok, mom.

Yes, good idea.

MAGIC WAY 3

Set rules and expectations ahead of time

All parents experience issues with temper tantrums or fights between children. When tantrums happen, parents often perceive their children to be unreasonable and struggle to figure out how to best respond to these challenging episodes. Unfortunately, most parents follow a reactionary approach, trying to find solutions only after the challenging situation has started.

Preventing a problem from happening in the first place is actually easier. Setting rules and expectations ahead of time with young children can help avoid these tantrums happening in the first place. Parents must become skilled at defining clear boundaries, rules, and consequences, as well as communicating their expectations clearly and explicitly to their children ahead of time.

Cartoon 8 shows how setting rules ahead of time can help sort out a tricky situation with kids playing loudly. Cartoon 9 also shows quick and easy ways to set expectations ahead of time to proactively prevent issues before they happen.

Cartoons for this Magic Way:

Cartoon 8: Set rules ahead of time and enforce with calm (kids playing loudly).

Cartoon 9: Easy ways to set expectations ahead of time.

Cartoon 8

Set rules ahead of time (kids playing loudly)

"So often, children are punished for being human. They are not allowed to have grumpy moods, bad days, disrespectful tones, or bad attitudes. Yet, we adults have them all the time."
Rebecca Eanes

Research behind the cartoon:

There is one universal truth about kids: they are noisy, which can be highly challenging for family members. To address this effectively, parents need to set clear expectations and consequences while using non-harsh, positive discipline practices. Providing expectations and consequences for behavior ahead of time also teaches children accountability and responsibility. The manner in which appropriate expectations are delivered is essential to achieving good outcomes. Diana Baumrind, a clinical psychologist known for her research on parenting styles, recommends a balanced "authoritative" parenting style[12]: authoritative parents set rules and limits and expect a high level of maturity and cooperation from their children. Contrary to "authoritarian" parents, "authoritative" parents offer children a lot of emotional support. For example, when children make mistakes, authoritative parents use an open conversation to help them understand what went wrong and explain the consequences of good and bad behavior. This warm, democratic parenting style, which balances authority with emotional support, is associated with a variety of positive outcomes, including increased school achievement and reduced risky behaviors (Steinberg, Elmen, & Mounts, 1989; DeVore & Ginsburg, 2005[13]).

Authoritative parenting is administered in a way that is firm and loving at the same time. Such discipline is also preventative, as it means ensuring that children know rules and consequences ahead of time (in cartoon: "Can you remind me what the rule is in the living room?"). Reviewing such expectations ahead of time serves two purposes: first, it can help avoid the problem altogether. Second, if the situation does arise, parents can refer back to the expectation while addressing the problem. When children do not follow family rules, we recommend that parents act not as tough disciplinarians but rather, as teachers. As our children's teachers, our goal is to calmly enforce rules and educate, but also give choices and positively reinforce good behaviors.

Noisy behavior can also occur when children are playing well together. Not such a bad thing! The fact that they are engaging in positive play should be rewarded (in cartoon: "You boys are doing such a great job playing together!"). While parents may want to address the noise level, they also want to continue encouraging creative play. To help accomplish this, parents can present choices or fun alternatives (in cartoon: "You can use your inside voice here, or go to your bedroom where you can be as loud as you want"). If kids are not allowed to be loud in certain areas of the house and need to go to their bedroom, reminding them of this rule should be carried-out calmly and without anger. With this method, both parents and children win: parents achieve their desired outcome without resentment and children continue to enjoy their boisterous fun!

Key take-aways to set rules ahead of time:

1) Make sure that children are aware of rules ahead of time, and agree that rules make sense. You can ask the children to describe the rules back to you to make sure they understand and know them.

2) Discipline positively. You are a teacher, not a punisher. Rules are created to protect everyone's safety and well-being, not to punish (in 'What to avoid' cartoon: "That's it. I'm taking the toys away").

3) When a child fails to abide by the rules, your job as a teacher is to give them reminders (in cartoon: "Can you remind me what the rule is in the living room?"). You can even exaggerate in a playful way ("oh nooo... someone forgot the rule!").

4) Suggest fun alternatives. This will help you avoid being perceived as the punisher. See Magic Way 2 for details.

Cartoon 8:
Set rules ahead of time and enforce with calm

What to avoid

✖ The mom is mostly relying on commands only ("Stop making so much noise").
✖ She reacts in an authoritarian way and punishes the boys by
taking the toys away, creating resentment and anger.

What Magic Mom would do

✔ The mom set the rules ahead of time so her children are not surprised.
✔ She connects in a positive way ("You are doing such a good job at playing together").
✔ She firmly, but patiently, reminds her children about the rules.
✔ She gives positive directions and options so the children feel in control.

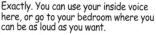

Cartoon 9

Easy ways to set expectations ahead of time

There are two easy ways for parents to proactively prevent issues in day-to-day interactions with their children by clearly and explicitly setting expectations ahead of time:

1) Show the way: show your child exactly what is expected of them instead of just asking them to do something. Too often, parents describe what they perceive to be simple instructions (in cartoon: "Be gentle with the pet" or "Be quiet") but children do not necessarily have a good understanding of what "gentle" or "quiet" really means to the parent in a specific situation. A child's understanding of being "quiet" can be very different from the parent's understanding. This is particularly true with young children (ages 2-5). Showing the way in a very explicit and obvious manner will leave no room for interpretation (in cartoon: "Be gentle... just like this...", and "Listen, this is how I whisper. Can you whisper?").

2) Rehearse ahead of time: setting clear expectations ahead of time can be a simple method to get the results you want, without the fights or the tantrums. Instead of trying to correct the child's bad behavior ("You are too loud" or "Your shoes are not on the shoe rack"), parents can simply identify challenging situations ahead of time, and remind their child about expectations (in cartoon: "Do you remember where to put your shoes inside?"). When kids know what is expected, they are more likely to deliver, and parents can avoid having to correct their child, which neither the parent nor the child will enjoy ("You forgot to put the shoes on the rack!"). A reminder ahead of time is more likely to elicit a positive action, and less likely to create resentment.

Cartoon 9 (part 1/2):
Show the way

A parent should demonstrate the expected behavior so the child concretely knows what to do. We often ask children to be "gentle" or to "whisper". Even if they understand the idea, they may not know what it means to "be gentle with a pet" or to "whisper to avoid waking the baby up".

What to avoid The mom asks her son to be gentle, but he doesn't know exactly what it means.	**What Magic Mom would do** The mom shows that being "gentle" means petting slowly and carefully.

What to avoid The mom asked her daughter to whisper, but the child is loud anyway.	**What Magic Mom would do** The mom and the child practice whispering together.

Cartoon 9 (part 2/2):
Rehearse ahead of time

Parents should be patient teachers who remind their children about expected behaviors ahead of time. Learning is a repetitive process and children often need several "reminders" to avoid getting in trouble. A child is more likely to accept a reminder than a rectification after the bad behavior has already happened.

Before getting to the table	Before getting in the car
Remember that we don't drop our food on the floor. Or what happens? — I have to pick it up.	We need to have fun in the car. Do you have your activity bag? — Yes!

Before walking past the baby's room	Before getting home
Remember that Sophie is sleeping. Can you show me your whispering voice? — This is my whispering voice.	Do you remember where to put your shoes inside? — On the shoe rack.

MAGIC WAY 4

Prevent tantrums before they start

Unfortunately, most parents follow a reactionary approach and try to find solutions only after a challenging situation has started. This results in parents constantly trying to address tantrums or resolve conflicts as they happen, multiple times per day. Because of this reactionary approach, these challenging situations keep happening again and again, pushing parents to the brink of mental exhaustion ("You can share this toy, it's not that complicated!").

Parents can work proactively to prevent some tantrums from happening altogether. Cartoons 10 and 11 present an easy step-by-step method to proactively identify and reduce tantrums and challenging situations. We will take the example of a family experiencing frequent fights between siblings over toys (cartoon 10) and challenging car rides (cartoon 11). Cartoon 12 gives simple examples of words you can teach children to help them prevent conflicts on their own.

Cartoons for this Magic Way:

Cartoon 10: Proactively prevent tantrums (fights over toys).

Cartoon 11: Proactively prevent tantrums (road rage).

Cartoon 12: Words to help children prevent conflicts on their own.

Cartoons 10 and 11

Identify root causes and proactively prevent tantrums and other issues

Research behind the cartoons:

Understanding the challenging situations that trigger tantrums and the specific skills that your child needs to learn to manage these situations are excellent starting points to proactively prevent tantrums. Ross W. Greene, Ph.D., author of "The explosive child"[14] recommends that parents identify:

1) the specific situations triggering the fights or tantrums ("root causes"). Most children are set off by the same five to ten conditions every week. Identifying these situations can help accurately predict and thus prevent tantrums.

2) the skills that children are lacking ("skill gaps"), which prevent them from responding to these situations in a more calm and measured manner. Greene writes that children who struggle the most "are lacking the skills of flexibility, adaptability, frustration tolerance, and problem solving skills most of us take for granted."

For example, parents with children who regularly fight over toys may find that the younger sibling is repeatedly stealing from the older one ("root cause"). The older sibling may lack the ability to come up with solutions to prevent this from happening ("skill gap"). Brainstorming solutions with the older sibling will be an excellent opportunity for the older sibling to improve this skill gap. Constructively coming up with solutions will also contribute to improving the child's emotional intelligence and social abilities.

Brainstorming solutions with a child is also one of the most effective parenting methods to proactively prevent future tantrums. Jane Nelsen, Ed.D. writes in "Positive discipline"[15] that "Adults don't realize how much they underestimate the ability of children to come up with solutions to problems and proposals they can live with. (...) Kids have ways of working things out that are both efficient and effective." The best method to reduce future challenging situations is often for both parents and children to sit down to brainstorm solutions together as a team.

Key take-aways to identify root causes and proactively prevent tantrums and other issues:

1) Identify the root causes of the issues: it could be that a sibling is regularly stealing toys or that car rides turn out to be very long and boring for children. Knowing and understanding root causes is the starting point for reducing challenging situations in your household.

2) Brainstorm solutions together: collaboratively work with children to come up with a list of possible solutions.

3) Identify skill gaps: does your child need to improve skills such as flexibility, adaptability, frustration tolerance, or problem solving? Think about the skills they need to de-

velop to manage similar challenging situations better.

4) Work with your child to proactively learn these skills.

Cartoon 10:
Proactively prevent tantrums (fights over toys)

Step by step method to proactively prevent fights

Understanding the situations that trigger tantrums or fights, brainstorming solutions with your child, and identifying skills your child needs to improve to manage these situations, are all excellent starting points to proactively prevent tantrums in your household.

1. Identify the root cause.
Find out what triggered the fight to avoid similar future tantrums.

She stole a toy from my bedroom. She does this all the time.

2. Brainstorm solutions.
Together, make a list of solutions (see next page for examples).

So, how can we prevent her from stealing toys from your bedroom?

3. Identify skill gaps.
Identify skills your child needs to better respond to similar situations.

Perhaps we can teach him strategies to remain calmer when his sister takes a toy.

4. Improve skills.
Teach your child how to best respond to similar challenging situations.

Imagine that one of your classmates takes a book from your desk. What would be a good way to respond?

Example solutions brainstormed with the children

Once the root causes have been identified (step 1), parents can now sit down with the children to brainstorm new solutions (step 2). Below are a few example solutions. Make sure you brainstorm with your children to find solutions that will work for YOUR family.

Solution 1: monkey lock.
The 5-year old will be able to open the door, but the 3-year old will not.

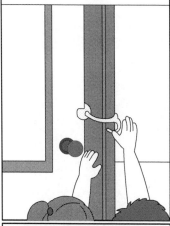

Solution 2: toy box.
Both children will get a toy box to protect their most precious toys.

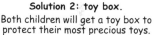

Solution 3: hard-to-reach spot.
The son can reach the top shelf to store his favorite toys.

Solution 4: patient teaching.
Teach the younger daughter to stay away from her brother's toys.

Cartoon 11:
Proactively prevent tantrums (road rage)

Two siblings often fight or have tantrums during car rides. After the ride is over, the mom will have a discussion with the children to identify the root cause of these tantrums and brainstorm solutions.

Step by step method to prevent future tantrums

Understanding the situations that trigger tantrums or fights, brainstorming solutions with your child, and identifying skills your child needs to improve to manage these situations, are all excellent starting points to proactively prevent tantrums in your household.

Example solutions brainstormed with the children

Once the root causes have been identified (step 1), parents can now sit down with the children to brainstorm new solutions (step 2). Below are a few example solutions. Make sure you brainstorm with your children to find solutions that will work for YOUR family.

Solution 1: new songs.
The mom created a new playlist with songs that both kids enjoy.

Solution 2: activity kits.
Activity kits include toys and books, and keep the children entertained.

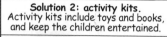

Solution 3: fun car games.
The mom found a few fun games to play in the car.

I can see a green car!

Solution 4: prepare for long trips.
Prepare more activities for long trips, ahead of time.

Cartoon 12

Words to help children avoid conflicts on their own

Fights and tantrums can often arise when children play together. Children may struggle to manage emotions and often lack the ability to communicate effectively with other children to find peaceful solutions. Not having the skills to navigate the complex world of social interactions leaves children with few tools to manage them. As a result, children may resort to physical responses such as screaming or pushing. Naturally, these responses tend to escalate conflicts and can result in full-blown fights, leaving parents perplexed as to how to help children through these conflicts.

Learning to avoid these conflicts in a peaceful way through calm communication is an important life skill that can be learned early. Parents can proactively teach their children to avoid conflicts on their own by using simple words or sentences such as "Please give my body space" or "Can I play with this toy?". By learning to use these simple words in common challenging situations, children may be able to avoid fights or tantrums on their own without parental intervention. Teaching these behaviors requires patience and persistence. However, these efforts will ultimately pay off with children developing important conflict resolution and social development skills.

Cartoon 12 presents four examples of simple words that parents can teach their children to avoid common conflicts.

Cartoon 12:
Words to help children avoid conflicts on their own

Parents can proactively teach children simple words or
sentences to help them avoid conflicts on their own.

To play with another child's toy.
Taking a toy from another child is one
of the most common reasons for fights.

Tim is using that toy. If you
would like a turn, you can say:
"When you are done,
please let me know."

To play with a friend.
Young children often struggle to
ask to play with a friend's toys.

Tim is using these cars
already. If you would like to
play with him, you can ask:
"Can we play together?"

To keep a toy for yourself.
Children often don't know what to
say when they don't want to share.

If another child wants to play with
your toy, but you want to play alone,
you can say: "I'm using this toy. I will
let you know when I am finished."

To get some alone time.
Children often struggle to leave
enough personal space when needed.

If you need space you can
say: "Please give my body space"
or you can choose to move away.

MAGIC WAY 5

How to motivate young children

Why is it so hard to motivate children to perform basic tasks such as getting dressed or brushing teeth? Parents often use rational arguments that make sense to adults ("Hurry up... We are late for school") but these arguments will do little to motivate young children. As a result, children may become frustrated and start a tantrum because they are now forced to do things they do not want to do.

Instead, you should speak to your child's heart and motivations. Most children just want to have fun and will respond better when parents find ways to make a situation more fun. Simple games, races, challenges or new interesting activities can do the trick and will help avoid arguments and tantrums. Both parents and children will have more fun in the process.

How am I going to motivate him to stop playing and go brush his teeth...

Cartoons 13, 14 and 15 show different "magic ways" to motivate a child to do basic tasks. These examples can help you understand what generally works best and inspire you to come up with your own games and challenges. Each child is different so you will need to find tricks that will work best for your child. Remember that the key is to make it fun and engage your child in a positive and entertaining way.

Cartoons for this Magic Way:

Cartoon 13: Motivate a young child to get dressed.

Cartoon 14: Motivate a young child to brush teeth.

Cartoon 15: Motivate a young child to use the toilet.

Cartoon 13:
Motivate a young child to get dressed

A dad needs to get out of the house soon, but his young son takes forever to get dressed. How can he help speed up the process?

4 easy ways to help a young child get dressed

Fun games will motivate a child a lot faster than orders ("Get dressed now!") or logical arguments ("We are late for school!"). The key is to make it fun and find out what works best for your child.

1. Count to 10.
Challenge your child to get dressed before 10. Start counting!

2. Race.
Challenge your child to a fun race (let him win).

3. Funny Act.
Be as creative as you can and make weird noises.

4. Promise a fun activity.
The child gets to do a fun activity when he is dressed.

Cartoon 14:
Motivate a young child to brush teeth

A mom wants to get everyone to bed. However, her little girl is not interested in brushing her teeth. How can the mom motivate her daughter?

4 easy ways to help a young child brush teeth

Fun games and activities will motivate a child a lot faster than orders ("Let's brush teeth now") or logical arguments ("We need to go to bed now, or we'll be tired tomorrow"). The key is to make it fun for your child.

1. Exaggeration.
Exaggerate or use a funny voice to draw your child's attention.

OOHHH I see very dirty teeth. eeew.... let's get them cleaned!

2. New fun thing.
Find an interesting way to brush teeth that is more fun.

Am I mixing mint and strawberry toothpaste? Well, yes I am.

3. Talking object.
Turn the toothbrush into a new fun toy.

I am Olivia the brush, and I brush everything... even your nose!

4. Promise a fun activity.
Promise a fun activity after your child is done toothbrushing.

I've got this new mint floss that we can use after brushing our teeth.

Cartoon 15:
Motivate a young child to use the toilet before bedtime

A dad struggles to go through the bedtime routine to get his 3-year old son to bed. The son wants to keep playing and does not want to start his bedtime routine.

Magic Dad's race to the toilet

To avoid an argument and potentially a tantrum, Magic Dad makes it fun. The dad knows that his son loves to race (as most children do) and challenges him to a race to the toilet. The end of the race results in laughter, with a friendly "challenge" to sit on the toilet first.

To highlight a sense of urgency for the child, the dad tells him:
"I am giving you a 3-second head start.
Go, go, go, 1... 2... 3..."

MAGIC WAY 6

How to use time-outs and discipline

In Magic Ways 1 to 5, we have reviewed strategies to defuse or prevent tantrums and other issues. However, parents using these strategies will invariably still experience challenging situations that these strategies will fail to resolve. When parents have tried to listen, understand feelings, affirm feelings and offer fun alternatives but the child is still in distress or misbehaving... is it time for time-outs or discipline?

Cartoon 16 presents a strategy for using time-outs effectively to help stop tantrums. In cartoon 17, we will review one more time the strategies we recommend to re-solve issues and avoid disciplining altogether, by trying to connect with your child and proactively find solutions. If all fails, we provide advice in cartoon 18 with four specific recommendations to make discipline work.

Cartoons for this Magic Way:

Cartoon 16: Using time-outs to stop tantrums.

Cartoon 17: Connecting before disciplining.

Cartoon 18: Disciplining effectively.

Cartoon 16

Using time-outs to stop tantrums

Research behind the cartoon:

The Magic Ways outlined earlier in this book (Magic Ways 1 to 5) are very effective in most situations, but will not prevent all tantrums all of the time. For more extreme tantrums or situations where tensions run high, young children might find themselves too overwhelmed with emotions. Listening, showing empathy and suggesting fun solutions might not be enough for parents to help defuse these tantrums. In these more extreme cases, parents have found success with time-out strategies. With time-outs, parents take their children to a "quiet zone" where the child has the opportunity to calm down and regain composure. A "quiet zone" is a safe area where children can retreat to cool down. Jane Nelsen, Ed.D. writes in her book "Positive discipline"[16] that "strong emotions can feel overwhelming to a young child. A positive time-out gives them an opportunity to calm down and catch their breath, so they are able to work with you to solve the problem." A quiet zone will help them become calmer in a safe place, without further engaging in fights or arguments.

But how can parents use quiet zones in an effective way? Thomas W. Phelan, Ph.D., author of "1-2-3 Magic"[17], recommends that parents calmly count to 3 before asking a child to go to their quiet zone. Counting to three gives children an opportunity to calm down and change their behavior. This method can be surprisingly effective. Here is how Thomas W. Phelan describes the process of counting to three, and enforcing the time-out when children continue their tantrums: "You hold up one finger, look down at your noisy little devil, and calmly say "that's 1". He doesn't care. He's insane with rage (...). You let five seconds go by, then you hold up two fingers and say "that's 2". That's all you say. But you get the same lousy reaction. So after five more seconds, you hold up three fingers and say "that's 3". Take five." In this case, the child did not stop the tantrum when the parent counted to three, so the child will need to go to their quiet zone for a time-out. We recommend that children stay in their quiet zone for 1 minute for every year of age (3 minutes for a 3-year old child, 4 minutes for a 4-year old child, etc). After a few minutes in their quiet zone and after regaining their composure, children can return to the original setting. Nothing is said about the argument or the tantrum, as it is not desirable at this point to get into a heated discussion again.

When parents first implement the time-out strategy, children may not be responsive to this new method and will continue their tantrums. This means that parents may need to use the quiet zone quite often in the first few days. However, after a few days, children will start understanding the consequences of their behavior, start calming down after "1" or "2" and be more open to a constructive discussion to find solutions to their problems. The time-out method gives parents an easy method to respond to tantrums that seem out of control. It also gives children an opportunity to understand that screaming or crying are not appropriate nor expected ways to behave. The method is not always easy to implement, and parents will need to enforce it consistently and persevere for a few days while the child learns this new system.

Key take-aways to using time-outs to stop tantrums:

1) Parents and children can build a "quiet zone". In this safe area, children can retreat to cool down and regain composure in situations where tensions run high.

2) Parents should count to 3 before asking a child to go to their quiet zone. Counting to 3 gives the child an opportunity to calm down and change their behavior.

3) At first, children may not be responsive to this new method and may continue their tantrums. However, after a few days, they will start understanding the consequences of their behavior, and will start calming down after "1" or "2". Initially, the process can feel a bit nerve-racking for the parents. However, parents need to remain consistent in their enforcement as everyone learns this new method and adapts.

Cartoon 16:
Using time-outs to stop tantrums

A 3-year old girl really wants to continue watching a cartoon, but her parents need to turn the TV off. The parents had set the right expectations and even used a timer to signal when TV time was over. However, the girl will have none of it and starts a tantrum.

How to use time-outs to stop tantrums (part 1/2)

For more extreme temper tantrums where the child does
not appear ready to calm down, time-outs can be effective.

Part 1/2...

Set expectations ahead of time.
Discuss the new time-outs and the
"1-2-3" time-out rule.

Jenny, we have a new rule. If you
start screaming and yelling, we
will say "that's 1". It's a warning
that you need to stop. If you
continue, we will say
"that's 2". If we get to
3, you will need to go to
your quiet zone.

Describe it back.
Your child needs to be able to
describe the new rule back to you.

Can you tell me
what I just said?

If I scream, you say
"1-2-3". If I still
scream at 3, I go
to my room.

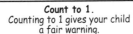

Count to 1.
Counting to 1 gives your child
a fair warning.

That's 1

NOOO I want
to watch TV.

Count to 2.
Counting to 2 gives your child
more time to calm down.

Ok, that's 2

It's not FAIR.
I want to watch
TV... NOW!!!

How to use time-outs to stop tantrums (part 2/2)

Time-outs are only effective if you follow basic rules,
such as as setting expectations ahead of time and
enforcing consistently for at least several days.

...part 2/2

Count to 3 - take five.
It's now time to go to the
quiet zone for a few minutes.

That's 3. Take five. Let's
go to your quiet zone.

ahhhh nooo......
I want TV....

After the time-out.
Nothing is said about the argument.
The child goes back to normal activities.

The first few days will be hard.
It will likely take a few days for your
child to understand the consequences.

Is this really working? Taking
Jenny to her bedroom is hard...

But one day...
Your child will eventually stop
the tantrum before you get to 3.

That's 2...

Ok, fine.....

Cartoons 17 and 18

Connecting before disciplining

Research behind the cartoon:

Proponents of positive discipline argue that punishments should not be used. Research shows that punishment is generally not the best way to solve problems, and we have offered in this book a variety of alternative strategies proven to be more effective (see Magic Ways 1 to 5). Parents often perceive punishment to be a good strategy because they think it will help their child experience consequences and learn from mistakes to avoid repeating the same behavior. However, the reality is that punishment is often accompanied by anger, and anger rarely works to convince a child that they should behave differently.

Research shows that punished children often build up resentment toward the punisher, with negative consequences including rebellion against parents (Nelsen, 2006[6]). Punishment remains a popular strategy with most parents, because it is an easy way to feel in control, even if it rarely works. We suggest replacing hard punishment and anger with:

1) Connecting and suggesting fun alternatives (as outlined in Magic Ways 1 to 5),

2) Respectful discipline, which defines firm boundaries and consequences ahead of time, in a positive and calm way.

Key components of respectful discipline include:

1) *Setting expectations ahead of time.* Discuss the consequences with your child before the events occur. The child should agree that the consequences are fair: the child can even contribute to deciding which consequences are appropriate. Parents should also keep consequences related to the offense (for example, a child cannot use their bike for a day if they forget to put their helmet on).

2) *Asking your child to describe the consequences back to you.* This is a very simple and helpful technique to verify that the expectations have been clearly set and understood by your child. You might find that your child was not listening at all, or did not understand the expectations. Clarify expectations until understood by your child.

3) *Enforcing in a calm manner.* If the negative event occurs (for example, a child hits a sibling), parents should firmly, but calmly, implement the consequence, as soon as the situation has calmed down and tensions are no longer running high.

4) *Enforcing consistently.* It is important to consistently enforce consequences when negative events take place.

Key take-aways to connecting before disciplining:

1) Anger and punishment rarely work as disciplining strategies.

2) Before implementing discipline, parents should first connect and use strategies from Magic Ways 1 to 5.

3) If all fails, parents should use respectful discipline as a calm way to set firm boundaries, without building resentment. This includes setting expectations ahead of time, asking the child to describe the consequences and enforcing the consequences consistently and in a calm manner.

Cartoon 17:
Connecting before disciplining

A 5-year old girl is often hitting her 3-year old brother. How can the parents approach the situation with the older girl? (note: this cartoon is focused on the older sibling, but parents should also follow Magic Ways 1 to 5 to help with the younger brother)

Connecting with the older child, before disciplining (part 1/2)

The dad connects with the older child and starts a discussion to brainstorm solutions. Note that this cartoon focuses on how the dad can work with the **older sibling** to find solutions, **before** having to discipline as last resort. (separately, the dad should also connect with the younger sibling to understand his actions - see Magic Ways 1 to 5 for recommendations)

Part 1/2...

Connecting with the older child, before disciplining (part 2/2)

The dad connects with the older child and helps her rebuild the castle.
Once tensions are no longer running high, the dad starts brainstorming
solutions to prevent these fights in the future (see Magic Way 4 for
example cartoons to work with your child to find solutions).

...part 2/2

* Refer to Magic Way 4 for example cartoons to work with your child to brainstorm solutions.

Cartoon 18:
Disciplining effectively

A 5-year old girl keeps hitting her little 3-year old brother despite her parents' best attempts to connect and find better solutions. Trying to work with both children to find solutions has only partially helped. How can the dad use discipline to help?

Magic Dad's essential steps to effective discipline

The dad has worked with both children to find solutions (see Magic Way 4 for example cartoons). The dad is now working on key steps to effective discipline to continue to help prevent these fights from happening.

BONUS CONTENT

Motivate and encourage self-esteem

As children become interested in various extracurricular activities, such as gymnastics, sports or music, they also experience fear, disappointment and frustration. These are all emotions that provide opportunities for growth and positive development. Parents who use positive parenting methods will raise their children in a way that empowers children to reach their full potential as resilient and fulfilled individuals.

The bonus cartoon shows an example of a challenging situation where a young girl is afraid of failing a gymnastics activity. The cartoon highlights how her mom understands her daughter's feelings and provides positive reinforcement to boost her daughter's self-esteem and confidence.

Cartoon for this bonus content:

Bonus cartoon: Motivate and encourage self-esteem.

Bonus cartoon:

Motivate and encourage self-esteem

"There are miracles and glory in every child. Our glory lies in empowering them to flourish their glory."
Amit Ray

Research behind the cartoon:

By promoting autonomy, parents support their children's individuality, empowerment and self-determination. In fact, autonomy-supportive parenting is associated with all sorts of positive child outcomes, such as increased school adjustment and psychosocial functioning (Joussemet, Landry & Koestner, 2008[18]).

Dealing with fears and challenges is a part of life; but when parents provide a combination of empathy and encouragement (in cartoon: "You've trained so hard, so give it everything you've got"), children develop the self-confidence to safely explore the world and try new things. Helping children soothe themselves during stressful times (e.g., by taking a deep breath) is also a good coping mechanism that kids can implement on their own in a variety of situations. When children deal with challenges, optimistic parents who remind children of their past successes, enhance their children's resilience while fostering belief in future endeavors (in cartoon: "Remember, last time you did great"). Such challenges also need to be approached with unconditional love, so children know that, regardless of mistakes, their parents will love them no matter what. This warm, loving and supportive parenting style improves children's confidence while empowering them with the knowledge and tools necessary to approach life as fully capable individuals.

It is also important for parents to point out that success comes from hard work and not just intelligence or talent. When children do well on a task, parents often say "You are so talented" or "You are so smart!". According to research by Carol Dweck[19], a professor of psychology at Stanford University, praising children for their natural ability can be counter productive. Once people start to think that success is linked to skills and talent (versus hard work), they tend to think that failures come from their lack of natural abilities. This often results in a person giving up early rather than persisting through difficulty.

Instead, praise your children for their hard work ("You have worked really hard to be able to do this"). Studies show that focusing on the effort and determination makes people better at overcoming future obstacles. However, Carol Dweck also points out that you should only give praise for hard work if hard work was indeed performed (empty praise is counter productive).

Key take-aways to encourage your child's self-esteem:

1) Empower your child and promote independence.

2) When doubt happens, encourage your child by reminding them of past successes (in cartoon: "Remember, last time you were stressed, but you still did great").

3) Success comes from hard work, and not just intelligence or talent. If your child has worked hard and does well on a task, be quick to praise them for their work (in cartoon: "You've trained so hard").

Bonus cartoon:
Motivate and encourage self-esteem

A young girl is afraid to fail at a gymnastic activity. Can her mom improve her child's confidence and get her interested in the activity again?

What to avoid

✖ The mom does not do a good job at recognizing the girl's emotions and concerns ("If you can't do it, it will be fine").
✖ The mom also unintentionally speaks negatively to try to influence her daughter to do better, but it results in the girl getting frustrated.

What Magic Mom would do

✔ The mom does a good job at listening to her daughter's concerns.
✔ She reminds her daughter of past successes, and speaks positively to help build her daughter's confidence and self-esteem.
✔ She praises her daughter's hard work, while providing emotional support.

Scientific research or books referenced in Magic Mom, Magic Dad

Magic Mom, Magic Dad distills the most important scientific findings into simple cartoons. Our PhD educated authors and contributors have used their background, personal experience with children, as well as extensive research, including the following references:

1   Five essential ingredients to effective communications: being aware of emotions; connecting; listening; naming emotions; and finding solutions: Gottman, J. (2019). The Gottman Institute: A research-based approach to relationships. Retrieved from https://www.gottman.com/parents/.

2   Listening with care and sensitivity shows kids that they are really being heard, which promotes children's emotional resilience. Wolin, S., Desetta, A., & Hefner, K. (2000). A leader's guide to the struggle to be strong: How to foster resilience in teens. Minneapolis, MN: Free Spirit Publishing.

3   Active listening is a key aspect of developmental parenting, which is believed to support many positive child outcomes. Roggman, L., & Boyce, L., & Innocenti, M. (2008). Developmental parenting: A guide for early childhood practitioners Baltimore, MD: Paul H. Brookes Publishing.

4   Talking to children about their worries shows em-

pathy and helps children verbalize their feelings. Durrant, J. E. 2016. Positive discipline in everyday parenting. 4th ed. Stockholm: Save the Children.

5   Responsive parenting has many wonderful benefits, such as more secure parent-child attachments, increased self-esteem, self-efficacy, and social development among children:

- Juffer F., Bakermans-Kranenburg M. & Van IJzendoorn M. (2008). Promoting positive parenting: An attachment-based intervention. New York: U.S.A.: Lawrence Erlbaum/Taylor & Francis.

-Laible, Carlo & Roesch, S. C. (2004). Pathways to self-esteem in late adolescence: The role of parent and peer attachment, empathy, and social behaviours. Journal of Adolescence, 27(6), 703-716.

6   Negative consequences of punishment may include resentment toward parents; revenge plotted to get back at parents; rebellion against parents; and retreat, that may involve becoming sneaky or experiencing a loss of self-esteem. Nelsen, J. (2006). Positive discipline. Retrieved from www.positivediscipline.com.

7   The 'incompatible alternative principle' of positive discipline. Kersey, K. (2006). The 101 Positive Principles of Discipline. Retrieved from https://ww2.odu.edu/~kkersey/101s/101principles.shtml.

8   Children are born altruistic. Godfrey, D. (2019). Retrieved from https://positiveparenting.com.

9   Supportive, involved parenting teaches social skills and is also associated with positive school adjustment and reduced behavior problems:

- Engels, R., Dekovic, M., & Meeus, W. (2002). Parenting practices, social skills and peer relationships in adolescence. Social Behavior and Personality, 30(1), 3-17.

- Pettit, G., Bates, J., & Dodge, K. (1997). Supportive parenting, ecological context, and children's adjustment: A seven-year longitudinal study. Child Development, 68(5), 908-923.

10   Love and Logic method described by Cline and Faye. Cline, F. & Fay, J. (2006). Parenting with love and logic: Teaching children responsibility. Colorado Springs, CO: NavPress.

11   Parents should stay out of squabbles unless absolutely necessary. McCready, A. (2019). Get your kids to listen without yelling, nagging, or losing control. Retrieved from www.positiveparentingsolutions.com.

12   Authoritative parenting is a parenting approach that includes a good balance of the following parenting qualities: assertiveness without being intrusive; supportiveness without being punitive; and demandingness while also being responsive. Baumrind, D. (1991). The influence of parenting style on adolescent competence and substance use. Journal of Early Adolescence, 11(1), 56-95.

13   A warm, democratic parenting style supports children's best interests without being permissive, and is as-

sociated with all sorts of positive outcomes for children and adolescents:

- Steinberg, L., Elmen, J. D., & Mounts, N. S. (1989). Authoritative parenting, psychosocial maturity, and academic success among adolescents. Child Development, 60, 1425-1436.

- DeVore, E. & Ginsburg, K. (2005). The protective effects of good parenting on adolescents. Current Opinion in Pediatrics, 17(4), 460-465.

14   Challenging kids are lacking the skills of flexibility, adaptability, frustration tolerance, and problem solving skills most of us take for granted. Greene, R. (2014). 'The explosive child : a new approach for understanding and parenting easily frustrated, chronically inflexible children'. HarperPb, 5th edition.

15   Adults don't realize how much they underestimate the ability of children to come up with solutions to problems and proposals they can live with. Nelsen, J., Lott, L., & Glenn, H. S. (2007). Positive discipline AZ: 1001 solutions to everyday parenting problems. Harmony, 3rd edition.

16   Encouraging time out provides a cooling-off period to help children feel better, because that is what motivates them to do better. It is important to get children involved in creating a space that will help them feel better. Nelsen, J., Lott, L., & Glenn, H. S. (2007). Positive discipline AZ: 1001 solutions to everyday parenting problems. Harmony, 3rd edition.

17   Parents can calmly count to 3 before enforcing a time-out. Phelan, T. W. (2016). 1-2-3 Magic: The new 3-step discipline for calm, effective, and happy parenting. Sourcebooks, 6th edition.

18   Autonomy-supportive parenting is associated with all sorts of wonderful child outcomes, such as increased school adjustment and psychosocial functioning. Joussemet, M., Landry, R., & Koestner, R. (2008). A self-determination theory perspective on parenting. Canadian Psychology, 49(3),194-200.

19   Praising children for their natural ability can be counter productive. Dr Carol Dweck, Ph.D, author of 'Self-Theories' (summarizes her research on the nature of achievement, motivation and success, Psychology Press; 1st edition, 2000) and 'Mindset: The New Psychology of Success' (examines people's reactions to failures, Ballantine Books; Illustrated Edition, 2007).

Magic Mom, Magic Dad Online

Follow us on instagram:
instagram.com/magic_mom_magic_dad

Follow us on Facebook:
facebook.com/MagicMomMagicDad

Made in the USA
Monee, IL
04 December 2021

83889695R00066